Spartan Discipline

Resist Temptations and Conquer Your

Long-Term Goals

Chris Thomson

Contents

"No one is free, if he cannot command himself"

-Pythagoras

Introduction

According to Greek mythology, Achilles was born to Peleus, king of Myrmidon. The people of Myrmidon were known as being fearless warriors. Achilles' mother, Thetis, was very concerned for her child's safety, so she decided to find a way to protect Achilles. She was very aware that her son would grow-up to be a warrior and fight in battle, so she attempted different techniques to make Achilles immortal.

When none of the techniques worked out, she resorted to going to the River of Styx, one of the several rivers of the underworld. The waters of this river could make a mortal being invincible. Thetis dipped her child into its waters, completely covering her son except for his heel from which she held on to him.

As Achilles got older, he became involved in the military. He fought in a number of battles, all of which he was victorious in winning.

Achilles would later meet his fate when, during a number of convoluted events, he was killed by his close friend,

Paris. The god Apollo guided Paris's arrow so that it hit Achilles in his one vulnerable spot, his heel. It is from this Greek myth that we get the phrase "Achilles' heel.

Though just a myth, the tale of Achilles is both relevant and accurate when describing the human condition. Each one of us has our own Achilles' heel, though our vulnerable spot is not our heels but our minds. When our minds are undisciplined, we suffer the consequences.

There is no problem that you can ever experience that is not a product of the mind. Nothing in life has inherent meaning to it; all meaning is created by the mind and is then projected on to life. In a study, two people rode a roller coaster, after which changes in their physiology was measured. The first person experienced fear during the roller coaster ride. For him, nothing about the ride was enjoyable. The physiology of this person showed all the signs of stress. The second person experienced the ride as being thrilling and very enjoyable. This person's physiologies showed all the signs of a person who was experiencing wellbeing. Both people experienced the same ride but reacted completely different; the only difference was the meaning that they gave to the experience.

When we lack self-discipline, we become a servant to our own minds. We obey its every whim. If we have a fearful thought, then we become the embodiment of fear. If we have an angry thought, then anger becomes the lens through which we view the world. If we have a thought of self-doubt, then that thought will become the qualifier from which we measure our potential.

It is bad enough for us to live with an undisciplined mind; however, at the collective level, our undisciplined minds create the world that our children will inherit. Violence, the destruction of the environment, poverty, racism, sexism, drug abuse, and the break-up of the family, are all symptoms of the collective undisciplined mind.

The only way to truly solve a problem is to attack it at its root, where it was caused it in the first place. For us, that place is our thoughts. When we develop self-discipline, we increase our awareness of the mind. With increased awareness of our minds, we can turn the tables on it.

Instead of being a servant to our minds, we become the master and of it.

Fortunately for us, we have a classic example of how to build self-discipline, the Spartans, a warrior society that enjoyed dominance between the 6th and 4th centuries B.C. This book will explore the fundamental principles that they observed that allowed them to be legendary warriors.

"All men's gains are the fruit of venturing." -
Herodotus

ONE

A Brief look into Sparta

Formerly known as Lacedaemon, Sparta was located on the Peloponnesus peninsula, southwest of Athens Greece. Sparta was unique in many of its achievements, including being the originator of the first functional democracy and a constitution that provided full power to an assembly of citizens. The Spartan government was complicated in that it was ruled by two kings, an assembly, and a council composed of 30 elders. The council, among its other duties, had the power to decide on laws that they deemed to be against the best interest of Spartan society. Additionally, it was the first Greek city- state to offer land reform, allowing the equalization of wealth among its people.

The population of Sparta was divided into three groups: Spartan citizens, the Perioikoi, and the Helots. The Spartan citizens lived within the city, served in the military, and were allowed to be involved in government decision making. The Perioikoi lived outside of the city in small villages. While enjoying freedom, they were not allowed to get involved in politics. Herlots occupied a social standing similar to that of serfs in that they were not slaves, and they could not own land. They held occupations that involved trade, skills, or mechanics.

The life of male citizens was devoted to military training. Military training began at age seven for Spartan males, but the selection of warriors began at birth when male newborns were evaluated for fitness. Babies that were deemed fit would be raised by the state, while babies that were unsuitable for future military service were discarded.

Military training lasted until age 30, upon which soldiers were granted full citizenship and voting rights. Known as Homoioi, these men would continue to serve the military in the capacity of the military reservist, which lasted until retirement at age 60.

While women were not involved in the military, they led active lives. Women were educated, were able to own property, enjoyed economic power, and were able to freely expressed their opinions. They were involved in athletic events, dancing, and singing. Spartan women enjoyed freedom from household duties as they were performed by the helot population.

Marriage was highly valued by the Spartan state as it relied on male children for the development of future warriors to replace those who died or retired. Males were allowed to marry upon reaching 20 years of age, while girls could get married at age 18. Given that males spent most of their life dedicated to the military, husbands and wives were separated most of the time. As the male population declined, due to death in battle, women's status in society became further elevated, eventually resulting in them being a dominant force in the Spartan economy.

The historical view of the Spartans is often distorted. The Spartans could not have achieved their success as warriors if the simplified historical accounts of their lives were accurate. While it is true that they were a warrior society, they were much more than that.

The secret behind the Spartan's success was that they were not one dimensional; they were multifaceted in their interest and pursued constant refinement of both their bodies and minds. They believed education should unite the body, mind, and spirit to overcome the problems that occur from the lure of fear, money, and sex.

Philosophy, music, dance, and poetry played a major role in Spartan life, and their philosophy was based on the heart and nature. The Spartans also were intellectually advanced in that they understood the importance of direct experience over secondhand knowledge.

Socrates considered the Spartans to be the most educated in philosophy and in speaking. The Spartans understood the importance of education and were a literate society. Agoge, the Spartan's version of public education, focused on developing both mind and body, stressing the cultivation of the intellect and verbal ability. Spartans were famous for their ability at rhetoric and wit. Socrates said of the Spartans: "the most ancient and fertile homes of philosophy among the Greeks are Crete and Sparta, where are found more sophists than anywhere on earth."

"If"

(Philip II of Macedon sent a message to Sparta: "If I invade Laconia you will be destroyed, never to rise again." The Spartan ephors replied with a single word: **"If."**)

TWO

Principles of the Spartan Warrior

$\mathbf{A}$ large part of Sparta's success was due to their observing fundamental principles that included honor, Know Thyself, nothing in excess, Keep the Measure, loyalty, love, perseverance, and selflessness.

Honor

When we think of honor, we often think of being the recipient of acknowledgment as when receiving an award; however, the Spartans held a deeper meaning for honor. For the Spartans, honor did not come from receiving recognition; rather, honor was the act of acknowledging the contributions of others, and it was sincere and heartfelt. Further, honor was independent of status or position.

The Spartan perspective of honor can be better understood using the example of a company. Imagine a company that has a CEO, the highest position within the company, a manager at the middle level, and a customer service representative at the bottom level.

The manager is keenly sensitive to the needs of the CEO and does whatever he can to make the CEO pleased with his performance. It is important to the manager to make the CEO happy because he understands that his job security is dependent on his performance.

When it comes to his relationship with the customer service representative, the manager expresses little interest in what he or she does as long as the customer service representative is doing their job.

Nowhere in this example does the manager express honor as the Spartans understood it. The only reason why the manager offers so much attention to the CEO is because the manager does not want to risk his job security. As for the customer service representative, the manager expresses little personal interest in them because the customer service representative does not fit into the equation of the manager's job security. As long as the manager ensures that the customer service representative is doing their job, the manager has accomplished what is expected from him.

If the manager demonstrated honor the way the Spartans did, this business scenario would go like this: The manager would honor the CEO because the manager has the understanding that the CEO is the commander of the company, and he is making all the decisions that will determine the success or failure of the enterprise. He honors the CEO by acknowledging his vital role in doing what is best for the company as a whole.

In the same manner, the manager honors the customer service representative because his or her role is as important as that of the CEO. The customer service representative is the face of the company; the first impressions that customers have of the company is based on their experience with this person. Just as with the CEO, the customer service representative is ensuring the success of the enterprise.

In the Spartan military, no soldier was seen as being superior to another soldier, regardless of their rank. It was understood that the success of Sparta was dependent on the loyalty of each soldier.   We can incorporate the Spartan sense of honor in our own life by giving sincere acknowledgment and appreciation to all members of our team, be they spouses, significant others, family members, friendships, co-workers, or employers.

Everyone in our life plays a role in shaping our life. Even those who may seem to be a thorn in our side contribute to our personal development for they, as do all of our relationships, function as a mirror to our minds and souls as they point out an aspect of ourselves we may be unaware of.

Know Thy Self

Of all the forms of knowledge that we pursue, the most important knowledge is awareness of the self. Without knowledge of self, all other forms of knowledge are at best flawed. The reason for this statement is that how we perceive anything in this world is dependent on our belief systems and learning.

Both our belief systems and our conditioning from the lens from which we experience the world. To have knowledge of self-involved knowledge of all aspects of self, mentally, physically, and spiritually.

Such knowledge was the foundation of education for Spartan youth. The people of Sparta, especially warriors and youth, pursued continuous and ongoing self-discovery in order to reach their highest potential, allowing them to contribute at the highest level to all of Sparta.

As a warrior, having self-knowledge is as important, if not more important, than knowledge of your enemy. Whether it is a war on the battlefield or in our daily life, unless we know what we are fighting for, unless we know how far we are willing to take our fight, unless we know how we want to conduct the battle, and unless we know what we are willing to lose, even if the battle is won we will be defeated by our oversight.

Knowing thyself is also critical because we can only change ourselves. That is one of the major flaws that occur between individuals or countries. Their motivation for war is to get the other party to change their ways.

Given each person or culture has its own unique perspective, it is unrealistic thinking to believe that imposing our will on others, in order to get them to undergo lasting change, will be successful. This fact has been repeatedly demonstrated throughout history; the war may have been won but unintended consequences always appear.

The challenge that we have as a society is that we do not encourage introspection. Our culture is one of the 24-hour media cycles, electronic devices, video games, and other forms of distraction. Our attention span is steadily declining, and our patience has grown thin. Anytime we engage in behavior that prevents us from taking a close inspection of our thoughts, emotions, and feelings, we create further distance from knowing ourselves. The Spartans understood this, which is why they placed so much emphasis on developing the mind and the practicing of silence.

The Spartans were well known as a culture of silence. Analysis of their speeches showed that the characteristic of their speech was one of being brief and meaningful; they used minimal words. This was part of their training as someone who is wounded in warfare would fare better if they were quiet and still versus being agitated. This type of philosophy runs parallel to monks, who take a vow of silence. Silence allows us to avoid getting caught up in our outer world and become more aware of our inner world.

Silence may have also benefited warriors on the physical level. Studies have shown that a person's physical pain lessens in its potency when the wounded person can remain calm. Spartans may not only have been brave on the battlefield, but they may also have experienced less pain when wounded. This claim is backed up by modern scientific studies in meditation, which shows that practicing meditation can reduces pain. Further, meditation is one of the most powerful ways to increase self-awareness.

Nothing in Excess

In Greek, the word "sophrosyne" makes reference to moderation, the ability to self-regulate, soundness of mind, and integrating with the soul. In modern times, the word that comes closest to the meaning of sophrosyne is moderation, or nothing in excess. The Spartans believed in not doing anything in excess, particularly when it comes to thinking, behavior, and desires. An example of this would be in their educational system. Though the Spartans were a warrior based society, children's education emphasized studying poetry, dance, and music.

Self-regulation, or self-control, was a skill that was highly respected in Spartan society. To have self-regulation is to be in command of our own minds and bodies. Self-regulation is inseparable from knowing thyself. The more we have self-awareness, the more capable we are in self-regulation. As in all of the principles that the Spartans observed in their daily life, self-regulation was practiced not for the good of the individual but rather the good of Spartan society. A great warrior is a master of knowing thyself and self-regulating, which makes him more likely to be victorious in defending his nation.

When we learn self-regulation or self-control, it naturally leads to the third quality of sophrosyne, which is a sound mind. Being self-aware allows us to self-regulate our thoughts, emotions, feelings, and actions. The ability to control our mind and bodies results in our soundness of mind.

Being of sound mind means we are not negatively influenced by our mental functions. A warrior that could overcome fear, rage, greed, or self-doubt was less likely to commit a form of action that went against the best interest of Spartan society.

Integration of the soul was the fourth and most important quality of sophrosyne. It referred to when a Spartan developed the recognition of spirit and the integration of spirit into daily life. For a Spartan to tap into his or her soul was to tap into the spirit or soul of Sparta. The Greeks had a word for the integration of the soul into the physical realm and that word was "Harmonia." Harmonia also is the source from where the word "harmony" is derived.

Harmonia refers to the uniting of individual parts to create the whole. The Greeks believed that harmonia has the power to reconcile the opposition that exists among the parts. By integrating the soul into daily activities, the Spartans believed that the person became greater than his mind and physical body alone. When all members of Spartan society achieved harmonia, then each individual became integrated with the spirit of Sparta. Harmonia is the next natural progression from having a sound mind.

In contemporary terms, we can achieve harmonia by developing contemplative practices that allow us to gain the direct experience of connecting with the non-physical aspect of ourselves, whether we call it spirit, soul, or consciousness. Practicing meditating, mindfulness, or any of the martial arts are excellent ways for reconnecting with the spiritual aspects of ourselves. The following is a simple technique for developing greater awareness to your non-physical dimension:

1. Find a quiet place to sit that is comfortable. Try to find a place where you will be free from distractions.
2. Close your eyes and allow yourself to relax.
3. As you breathe normally, place your awareness on your breath, following it as it flow into your body during inhalation and out of your body during exhalation.
4. As you follow your breath, you will most likely experience your mind wandering. When this

happens, simply return your attention to your breath.

It is important not to judge yourself, regardless how often you lose your concentration. Do not judge anything that you experience, nor should you try to control anything. Whatever you experience, allow it to occur.

5. As you develop a greater concentration in following your breath, your mind will start to become calm. When you reach this stage, place your attention on any thoughts that should arise. Can you find the place from which the thought appeared? After a period of time, the thought will fade away. Can you find where it went?

6. Now pay attention to another thought and follow it until it fades away. Before the next thought arises, what do you notice? What do you see?

Practice this exercise daily until you become proficient. Keep practicing until you can not only find that place between thoughts, but you can spend time there. This space between your thoughts is the portal to your non-physical self. You can call it your spirit, your soul, or pure consciousness. Either way, it is this aspect of the self, when cultivated, that leads us to what the Greeks referred to as harmonia.

Keep the Measure

The term "Keep the Measure" refers to how all forms of diversity are expressions of, and permeated by the essence of life. It is a concept that dates back to the ancient Pythagoreans and the god Apollo. It can be a difficult concept to understand; however, the impact of understanding this can be life changing.

Consider a symphony with all its musicians and their various instruments. Each instrument produces its own distinct sound. When all the musicians play together, all sense of distinction between the different sounds disappears as the sounds blend together.

Another example would be how the rivers of the world may appear as separate entities until they flow into the ocean. Once they enter the ocean, all sense of individuality or separateness disappears as they merge into oneness.

Going back to the metaphor of the ocean, a drop from the ocean may seem insignificant when compared to the ocean itself; however, the drop contains the exact same composition as the ocean. Any weaknesses or flaws that you perceive yourself as having is just illusionary. The essence of who you are is of the same nature as that from which the entire universe was created.

We experience ourselves as being separate from the rest of the world, not seeing how this sense of separation is illusionary. Look around you, and you will see a variety of objects in your environment. You may see furniture, cars, trees, other people, and so on. From our perspective, each of these objects appears to be a separate entity onto itself. It seems obvious that a piece of furniture is not a car or that a tree is not a person. However, to perceive objects in this manner is not accurate; it only seems that way because of the way our conceptual mind works.

Anything that we can perceive, with the exception of sound and light, is made of atoms. Discoveries in quantum physics have revealed that the atom is not a solid object as once thought. Rather, the atom is composed of subatomic particles that are separated by vast distances of space. In turn, these subatomic particles are made up of even smaller particles. If we were able to drill down through these sub-particles, we would eventually find energetic space. In other words, physical form and solidity are just an illusion. At the subatomic level, a brick is no more solid than the evening sky.

Everything that we can ever experience in life is a physical manifestation of pure energy. The diversity of the world is the expression of a single oneness that has been referred to as the quantum field, consciousness, or god. This is captured in the ancient expression, "This is that, that is that, and that is all that is." For this reason, the phrase "Keep the Measure" is deeply tied to sophrosyne, the integration of spirit into daily life. The concept of "Keep the Measure," reinforced the idea that regardless if they were Spartan citizens, peroikoi, or Helots, each person was a vital component of the Spartan state.

The concept of Keep the Measure reminds us that everything is life is intimately connected to a common source that is unperceivable to our limited minds. It also reminds us that, contrary to how most of us experience the world, that it is impossible to take action toward others without it impacting ourselves.

In order to make Keep the Measure relevant in your daily life, you will first need to convert this idea from an intellectual understanding to becoming your own direct experience. Learning meditation or other contemplative practices can make this possible. Until then, start making it a habit of reminding yourself that nothing in your experience of life is separate from yourself.

Loyalty

For a Spartan, it was expected that loyalty to the state supersedes everything else. It was this sense of loyalty that made the Spartans such a formable force on the battlefield. In the same manner, a sense loyalty is vital in developing self-discipline. Without a sense of loyalty, developing self-discipline is like building a sand castle on at the edge of the surf. As soon as an obstacle or challenge sneaks into our life, we will most likely slip into reaction mode and forget about anything that we learned about self-discipline.

When we develop a sense of loyalty for another, that loyalty becomes like an anchor as we now have something to fight for. For the Spartans, loyalty was vital for their success as it provided the cohesiveness that allowed them to be the formable warriors that they were.

Loyalty is also one of the dominant themes in Homer's epic poem, the Odyssey. The Odyssey tells about the journey home of Odysseus, the king of Ithaca. Odysseus was returning home after spending the last ten years engaged in the Trojan War. During that ten year absence, the wife of Odysseus, Penelope, did not even know if her husband was alive. During his absence, Penelope stayed loyal to her husband, even though she was visited by suitors. Telemachus, the son of Odysseus, stood-up to the suitors. Eurycelia, the nurse of Odysseus, maintained her loyalty to Odysseus by remaining with Penelope.

Loyalty can be cultivated by following basic principles. Learn to be honest with people. It is impossible to be perceived as being loyal if your honesty is in question. Learn to become impartial when dealing with others. Rather than judging others, practice being objective and accepting of others.

When it comes to those close to you, do not make your relationship as being conditional. Loyal relationships do not set up conditions that need to be met. Loyal relationships are unconditional.

While loyal relationships are not conditional, it does not mean you blindly accept what the other person is doing. For this reason, it is important to establish boundaries. Honoring one's self is essential before we can offer loyalty. I am loyal to my spouse and pose no conditions on her for my love. On the other hand, if she was ever to do something that would harm me, I would think of my safety first.

Love

You may be surprised reading that love was among the essential principles that made Spartan warriors successful on the battlefield; however, with further analysis, it makes sense. It may sound trite, but it is true; the greatest force for overcoming fear is love. In the warrior society, this was exemplified by the love felt by an individual warrior for his fellow warriors. During a battle in Thermopylae, the Spartan army experienced significant loss, and the few remaining soldiers were left facing their inevitable death by the enemy. One Spartan soldier asked his platoon commander as to what thoughts he and his fellow soldiers should hold during their last minutes of life. The commander told them to fight on for the love of their comrades.

Love is essential for developing self-discipline. Without love, our focus is on ourselves. Anytime we focus on ourselves; we become ensnared by the egoic mind. The ego' sole function is self-preservation, and self-preservation is a reaction to fear. When we have the love for another, our attention shifts from ourselves to the one we love, and we reduce the influence of the ego.

Problems with self-discipline are rooted in fear, the fear of failure or the fear of the unknown. If I am undisciplined, it is because either I have a fear of failing in my efforts to take responsibility, or I am fearful of what may happen if I do take action. Instead of experiencing a sense of uncertainty, I may choose not to take action because it feels safer. When I feel love for another, I am more likely to take action, especially if I feel it would be impactful for my loved one. The Spartans understood that love is the source of courage.

Perseverance

An enduring theme in Greek mythology is that of perseverance, and a classic portrayal of perseverance is from the Odyssey. Odysseus's epic challenges include being held the prisoner, endless battles with the opposition, and numerous temptations for an easier or more pleasurable experience. At the same time, his wife Penelope faithfully waits ten years for his return from war, even though she had no knowledge if he was even alive. To persevere means to continuously advance forward in life regardless of the obstacles, challenges, hardships, or perceived failures that are encountered along the way.

A true hero or warrior can only be so because they have been able to persevere. The quality of perseverance is intimately connected with the quality of Know Thyself and Keep the Measure. As a review, Know Thyself refers to having intimate knowledge of our own thoughts and beliefs. What determines if we persevere or not is based on our beliefs. If we believe that it is too difficult to accomplish our goal, then we will not make the necessary effort to accomplish our them. Conversely, if we believe that we can succeed, despite the difficulties or obstacles, we will continue to exert ourselves, which vastly improves our chances for success.

Keep the Measure, which refers to the diffusion of all diversity into the creation of unity, is a profound concept. If understood, it will create instant perseverance in you, as will all the principles discussed in this book. Understanding Keep the Measure is best accomplished through a contemplative practice, such as meditation. I offer the following exercise to you so that you have the opportunity to experience a glimpse of what I am talking about. To do this, do the following:

1. Find a quiet place where you can sit with minimum distractions.
2. Sit down and allow yourself to become comfortable.
3. Close your eyes and place your attention on your breath as you breathe normally.
4. Focus on your breath during inhalation; feel the sensations as you follow your breath as it courses through your body during inhalation.

5. When you exhale, feel the sensations as you follow your breath as it courses through your body during exhalation.

6. Continue to observe your breath for as long as you can.

7. As you observe your breath, you will experience thoughts, sensations, sounds, and other sensory information. Allow all of these phenomena to appear in your awareness. Do not try to control them. Do not try to resist them. Do not try to analyze or modify them with your imagination. In fact, do not do anything. Whatever happens, let it happen. Whenever you find your mind wandering, gently return your attention back to your breath.

8. As you continue to develop greater skill in observing your breath, you will notice that it takes less and less effort to observe it. When this happens, simply allow yourself to observe all the phenomena that appear in your awareness.

9. When you are able to stay as the observer of all phenomena without engaging any of them, pay attention to the silence and stillness within you. When you find this place, allow yourself to increase the amount of time that you spend there.

10. Now try to locate the one who is aware of thought, sensation, and other phenomena. Regardless of what answer you receive, repeat the question by asking yourself "And who is the one that is aware of that?" Challenge the answers that you receive by continuing to ask "And who is aware of that?"

Every answer you give must refer to something that is phenomenal. In other words, we can only know that which we experience through thought, perceptions, hearing, smelling, or feeling. In order for there to be an object, there must be an observer. Thus, regardless of your answers to the question, it cannot be you. You cannot be both the object and the observer at the same time.

I share this with you, not as some metaphysical or philosophical exercise; it is much more than that. If you are patient and persistent in practicing this exercise, you will eventually come to the profound realization that the true nature of who you are is beyond anything that you can experience. This is why the Spartan Warriors balanced their fighting skills with principles such as Keep the Measure; these principles are intended for developing greater awareness to our true identity, which is beyond the limited definitions that are created by our minds. This understanding is what made a warrior truly great, as with this understanding they were able to transcend the forces that most warriors succumbed to.

Selflessness

The last principle that we will discuss is that of selflessness. In a way, selflessness encompasses all of the previous principles that have been discussed. Plutarch, the ancient Greek historian, once asked a commander of the Spartan army as to why soldiers are fined for losing their spear or helmet but are put to death for losing their shield. The commander explained that the loss of a helmet or spear puts the soldier at risk, while the loss of a shield poses risk to every soldier on the line. The act of selflessness was also demonstrated when an army of Spartan warriors was crossing a vast desert, desperate for water. A group of scouts that went searching for water returned with news that they found a stream. They approached Alexander, their king, with a helmet that they had filled with water and offered it to him. Alexander expressed his gratitude to the scouts and proceeded to dump the water on the ground. Alexander understood that a cohesive unit requires selfless action. Had he drunken the water, he would have risked losing that cohesiveness, which was so vital to success. In the next chapter, we will discuss how to incorporate the principles from this chapter

"The Spartans do not ask how many are the enemy, but where are they." - Plutarch

THREE

Developing a Plan for Self-Discipline

The Oxford Dictionary defines self-discipline as: "The ability to control one's feelings and overcome one's weaknesses; the ability to pursue what one thinks is right despite temptations to abandon it." The principles that we discussed in the previous chapter are excellent for developing self-discipline. Before discussing how to incorporate these principles into a plan of action, it is vital to first examine the forces that drive human behavior.

The reason why Spartan warriors were so formable and efficient on the battlefield had nothing to do with the weapons they used, nor did it have anything to do with the size of their army, which was of only moderate size. What distinguished the Spartans from other armies was their mindset. To better understand this mindset, we need to discuss some basic psychology.

The human mind operates on two primary forces that influence all of our behaviors. These forces are our desires for positive experiences and our desire to avoid negative experiences. We are hardwired to interact with our world based on these two forces. What determines a positive experience or negative experience is determined by culture, up-brining, and individual experience. While most of us experience the death of someone we love as negative, some cultures celebrate death as they believe that the deceased will be moving on to the next plane of existence.

You may have been raised by your parents to believe that taking risks should be avoided at all cost, while some people were encouraged to take risks.

As previously mentioned, someone who has problems with self-discipline has learned from past experience that taking action had to move negative associations to it than positive ones. Perhaps this person experienced criticism in the past when they took action, which led to self-doubt.

Since we avoid negative experiences, it would be expected that this person would be hesitant to take action in the future. When we are afraid to take the necessary action to advance our life forward, we begin to erode our self-esteem.

What changes a person is new experiences. A person who considers themselves shy, and does not want to attract attention to themselves, does so because they want to avoid the negative experience of what may happen if they opened themselves up to others. Yet, this same person may one day find themselves being part of a play or a recital and experience the enthusiastic response of the audience, while developing a whole new association as to what it means to receive attention.

The principles that were discussed in this book are powerful because they redirect our attention from ourselves to something that is bigger than us, which leads to a sense of connection. Whether it is our loved ones, an organization, the country that we live in, or the universe itself, we all need to be able to connect to something larger than ourselves. When we are able to do this, our sense of connections becomes more powerful than the egocentric functions of the mind. It is from this position that self-discipline is born. Self-discipline is the force that gets us to do the things that are needed in order to create value for others and ourselves.

Since the only action that we can control is the action that flows from ourselves, self-discipline exerts itself in two ways. The first way is that action that is derived from self-discipline flows directly to, and benefits, the ones that we wish to serve. The second way is that action derived from self-discipline benefits us. Because we benefit from the action, we expand in our potential and are able to offer others even greater value. For this reason, we can think of ourselves as a battery, and self-discipline is the electrical charge. With a weak electrical charge, a battery is ineffective in providing the power that is needed to make a vehicle operate. However, when a battery is fully charged, it retains the potential to power not only the vehicle but to sustain its own life.

When we become connected to someone or something outside ourselves, that sense of connection amplifies our experience. The object of our connection becomes an extension of us. We become motivated to behave in a way that leads to positive experiences for ourselves and others. Given this understanding of the importance of connection, we will now discuss how to apply the principles to your daily life so that you can expand your sense of connection with others as well with yourself.

Honor

1. Determine who or what do you experience a connection with? Is it another person? Is it an animal? Is it a group, nature, spirit, or god? Once you have identified the object of your connection, write down all the reasons why you feel connected to it. Does the object of your connection provide you with a sense of belonging? Does the object of your connection make you feel understood? Perhaps your object of connection inspires you. Make a list of all the ways the object of your connection benefits you.

2. Write down all the reasons why you honor this person or thing? What is it about them that you admire or appreciate? By identifying your reasons

for honoring them, you will strengthen your connection with them.

3. Make a list of all the ways you can express your appreciation to the object of your connection. Perhaps it would be expressing your gratitude. Maybe it involves helping them lighten their load by taking on some of their responsibilities. If nature is your source of connection, what actions can you take to protect it? If it is god, what can you do to honor him or her? If it is someone who is deceased, what could you do to honor their memory? When you have a list of the ways you can honor your object of connection, make a commitment to yourself that you will put one of your ideas into action.

Know Thyself

The principle of Know Thyself requires honest self-reflection. As mentioned before, our behavior is guided by our expectations of what we will experience. If we believe that our actions will lead to a positive experience, we will most likely engage in it. If we expect a negative experience, we will most likely avoid taking action.

Commit to making a contemplative practice a part of your daily routine. Journaling, meditation, mindfulness practices and spending time in nature are all invaluable in developing self-awareness. Regardless of the contemplative practice that you decide upon, do the following exercise. It will lead to personal insight, which then can be expanded upon by the contemplative practice that you choose.

1. Determine what has prevented you from being self-disciplined in the past. When you have identified the reasons for your lack of self-discipline in the past, make a list of all the consequences that you experienced in your life for not being self-disciplined. Make your list as long as possible.

2. Make a separate list of all benefits that you could experience if you did exercise self-discipline; this list should be longer than the list of the consequences of not taking action.

3. When you have completed both lists, review them, making sure that you allow yourself to experience the emotions that you feel as you read it. Keep this list and review it twice daily, once in the morning and one in the evening. Do this over the period of three weeks.

Nothing in Excess

In order to address the principle of Nothing in Excess, take a close inspection of your life. Where in your life do you not exercise moderation? Do you sleep too much, party too much, watch too much television, or spend too much time playing video games? Perhaps you make too many excuses or worry too much. Identify all the ways that you engage in excess. When you have identified the way you engage in excess, think of alternative ways of behaving that will create more balance. In other words, if you spend too much time playing video games, what could you do instead? Could you read, take a walk, or talk to a friend? Make a list of alternative behaviors that you can pick and choose from. Make sure that you select activities that you enjoy doing.

Keep the Measure

As for the principle of Keep in Measure, look for a way that you can connect with the Source of all that is. Whether it is a religious teaching, a spiritual or metaphysical teaching, or being in nature, find a practice for yourself that connects you with life, a practice that resonates with you. If you already have a spiritual or religious practice that is meaningful you, find ways to get more involved with it. When choosing a practice, get curious and do not restrict yourself to the obvious choices. Learning meditation, yoga, and martial arts can be a powerful spiritual experience.

Loyalty

Remembering that the principle of loyalty involves being honest with people, being impartial, and establishing boundaries for yourself. If you have difficulties with any of these areas, start developing yourself by finding resources or strategies for their development. There is a wealth of resources that are available that provide techniques for improving in all these areas. Do not limit yourself to books or CDs. Consider workshops or find a mentor. If you know someone who is strong in these areas, learn from their experience. Also, use the exercise under the section **Know Thyself** by applying it to loyalty, or any of the other principles, so that you can become more fully aware of the consequences for not advancing in these areas and the benefits of doing so.

Love

For the principle of Love, you are going to take a different approach as your goal for this exercise is to develop a greater love for yourself. Most people are able to express love for others; however, many people have difficulty experiencing love for themselves. Ultimately, we cannot truly love others without first learning to love ourselves; it is critical that you be able to acknowledge your own self-worth.

All change in behavior occurs as the result of changing the meaning that we associate with the behavior. If I have a problem with self-discipline, it is because I associate having a lack of self-discipline as being more positive than taking action and seeing it through.

In the exercise for the Know Thyself section, you were asked to create a list of all the consequences that you experienced due to having a lack of self-discipline and a list of all the positive experiences you would experience for taking action. The purpose of this exercise was to cause you to focus on all the negativity that comes from not being self-disciplined and all the positives for changing this mindset. By rewarding yourself, you will create a change in the meaning that you associate with being self-disciplined.

In order to keep the change process moving forward and not retreating back to your old behavior, it is important to reward or reinforce any behavior that moves you closer to your goal. Because of this, your job is to create a list of all the ways you can reward yourself for initiating action that brings you closer to your goal.Your list should have a variety of ways that you can reward yourself.

When reinforcing yourself, it is important to do so at the moment you catch yourself moving in the right direction. By doing so, your brain will associate taking action with receiving a reward. If your list includes going to the movie theater, you will most likely not be able to implement that reward until some time later. If you do have such rewards on your list, then make sure you find a way to reward yourself right away with a smaller reward, then reward yourself with the larger reward when you are able to take advantage of it.

Perseverance

In order to implement the principle of Perseverance, remember your lists that you made for the principle of Know Thyself. Perseverance occurs when we constantly keep in mind the positive experiences that we will enjoy for sticking with our plans and the negativity if we do not. Really reflect on the negativity that you are creating for yourself and others by not practicing persistence. Conversely, reflect on what being successful would mean for you and those that you care about.

Selflessness

The final principle of selflessness is more of a byproduct of all the other principles. When we practice honoring others by recognizing their contributions to others, we not only acknowledge them for their efforts, we allow ourselves to get inspired to live up to our potential.

When we Know Thyself, we develop and understanding of how our own mind works so that we can take charge of it, rather than allowing it to take charge of us. When we practice nothing in excess, we keep ourselves balanced by not get caught up in extreme thinking or behavior.

When we develop and understanding of Keep the Measure, we stop feeling like that we are alone in life or that we are somehow separate from others. Rather, we gain an understanding that we and all of the rest of life are interdependent and are connected to each other. In this manner, the principle of Keep the Measure is consistent with the concept of karma or the "golden rule."

What we do in life has a ripple effect on life itself. It is impossible to do anything in life without it reverberating through all of life. The consequences of our actions may not appear immediately; but, they will appear eventually. When we practice loyalty, we move from being focused on our own egocentric needs and invest ourselves in the wellbeing of others. When we open up our lives to love, we not only forge a connection to others but summon the motivation to challenge our own sense of limitations in order to protect our beloved.

By developing perseverance, we can maintain our efforts regardless of the challenges that we may face. All of these principles culminate in creating the quality of selflessness. When we are selfless, we are more concerned about the welfare of others than that of our own lives. Because of this, we explode in our potential as human beings as we discover qualities and abilities within ourselves that we were unaware of. In turn, these qualities and abilities may become more fully developed, leading to further breakthroughs and even more discoveries. We find ourselves caught in an upward spiral of success as we exceedingly contribute to others while reaping the benefits of the continuous expansion that becomes our life.

The power to transform our lives by adopting the principles used by the Spartans, and applying them to our lives daily, provides us with a whole new perspective of that which we refer to as "self-discipline." When we were growing up, we may have been told of the importance of self-discipline; but, we most likely were never provided a context that would allow us to develop a sense of appreciation for it. Too many of us never understood that developing self-discipline could be life transforming.

If you have problems with self-discipline, my hope is that you will get inspired by the possibilities that these Spartan principles hold for your life.

"Add a step forward to it."

(A Spartan mother to her son when he complained his sword was too short.)

FOUR

Spartan wisdom and Goal setting

The principles and beliefs of Spartan society provided a solid foundation for success both on and off the battlefield. For most of us, life will never be as rigorous as it was in Spartan society, especially for males. The beliefs and principles that they lived by are the reasons for their claim to fame in the history of warfare. Interestingly, many of the Spartan principles and values that were key to achieving their goals have shown up in modern day research on goal setting. *There are extra pages at the end of the book for you to perform the excises within this chapter or notes in general*

Goal Assessment

One of the best predictors of goal achievement has to do with how meaningful the goal is. The following sections on legacy and ownership will explore that more deeply. But before we do so, it is valuable to create a profile or snapshot of your life so that you can better assess where you are in your life right now. The only way you can get somewhere else is to first determine where you are right now.

The following exercise can be done in the form of a chart, graph, or in writing. First, think of all the areas of your life. The most common areas are Relationships, professional, financial, physical health, emotional, and spiritual. If you want, you can break these areas down even further, for example, Relationships could be broken down to a spouse, parent, and friend. Professional could be broken down to Leader, professional development, and mentor.

The idea is to list all the areas in your life and rate them on a scale from 1-5. This scale relates to your level of fulfillment within that area. The difference between the score you give yourself and the number 5 represents the amount of improvement that you need focus to on. For example:

- Relationships: 3
- Professional: 3
- Spiritual: 5

- Emotional: 4
- Physical Health: 2

The identification of the different areas of your life, and the ranking of them provides greater precision for the development of meaningful goals. This process correlates with the ethos of the Spartans. They valued accuracy and simplicity. These qualities are consistent with the exercises in this book.

Based on this profile, I score very high on spiritual and emotional matters; however, my physical health could use work, and there is room for improvement in my relationships and in my professional life. Knowing this, I would set goals for myself in these two areas. In order to do this, I would ask this question to myself: "What would I need to achieve in order for me to feel more fulfilled in _____? I would ask this question for all areas that I want to improve. Once you have identified the areas of your life that you want to improve on, the next step is to refine your goals.

When refining your goals, it is important to observe the following points:

- Level of Difficulty
- Written
- Specific
- Measurable
- Timeline
- Outcome and Process

Level of Difficulty

When choosing a goal, research shows that the best goals are difficult yet attainable. If the goal is too easy to accomplish, then the level of performance will be low. If the goal is seen as being too difficult, performance will gradually decline due to frustration and doubt. Choosing goals that are difficult but attainable are shown to yield the highest levels of performance.

Written

When identifying your goals (or doing any of the exercises in this book), it is very important to write them out. The process of writing rewires the brain in a manner that enhances awareness.

Specific

When writing your goals, they need to be specific. For example:

- I want to increase my income
- I want to learn to relax
- I want to spend more time with my family

All of these goals are very general and are ineffective for generating the kind of action that leads to success. Remember the Spartan value of precision; you need to write out your goals with precision. For example:

- I want to increase my income by 20%.
- I want to reserve 30 minutes a day doing things that I find relaxing.
- I want to devote 10 hours a week focusing on being with my family.

Notice how these goals are much more specific than the original examples. Not only they are more specific; they meet the third criteria: They are measurable. It is very easy to determine if progress is being made toward these goals. I can tell when I have reached a 20% increase in my income. I can tell if I am spending 30 minutes relaxing, and so on.

Finally, your goals need to have a timeline. We need a time frame for achieving our goals; otherwise, we will not have the kind of focus that is needed for success. For example:

- I want to increase my income by 20% within two years.
- I want to reserve 30 minutes a day doing things that I find relaxing for a period of one month.
- I want to devote 10 hours a week focusing on being with my family for a period of one month.

So far, you have identified the areas in your life where you want to set goals. You also have learned how to write effective goals. The next step is to identify outcome and process.

Outcome

Outcome refers to the final result that you are looking to achieve, while process refers to the strategies, skills, or knowledge base that you need to achieve the goal. Your outcome is the same thing as your goal. The reason why the word "outcome" is used is that outcome is more easily associated with the final result, of what it "looks like."

One aspect of goal setting that is often overlooked is the power of the mind to develop an image and to expand our awareness to that which is consistent with that image. We can illustrate this by using the making of a sandwich as an example. Imagine that you are not really hungry but you take a peek into your refrigerator anyway. As you look inside the refrigerator, there may be numerous food items in it, but none of them grab your attention. You simply give them a brief glimpse then continue to look around.

Now imagine a different scenario where you are hungry for a sandwich. Your thoughts are on the sandwich; you have memories of sandwiches that you had in the past, and you can even remember the taste of your last sandwich. Unlike when you were not hungry, you know have a vivid experience in your mind of a sandwich. Now when you look inside the refrigerator, any possible ingredient for your sandwich will receive your full attention.

This is the power of taking your goals and imagining them as future outcomes. Take time each day to imagine what your goal would look like if it was fully manifested right now. Involve as many senses that you can when you imagine it. See in your mind. If it existed right now, what would it sound like? What would it feel like? What would it smell like? What would it taste like?

If you do this every day, those people, places, or things that are consistent with achieving your goal will attract your attention.

Process

Process refers to the skills, knowledge, or steps that are needed in order to achieve your goal. If your goal is to go back to school, what is the process that you would need? The most effective way to do this is to brainstorm a list. For example, if my goal is to go back to school, my list may look something like this:

- Identify colleges that I am interested in
- Research the colleges for academic programs, cost of tuition, and so on
- Contact the admissions office
- Get copies of my transcripts from my previous schools

- Schedule an appointment with an admissions representative
- Obtain a college catalog
- Identify student loan or scholarship options
- Start a saving account for school expenses

When writing your list, write everything that comes to mind, even those things that seem irrelevant. The idea is to empty your mind as you write your list so that you do not miss anything. Going back to the Spartans, from the time they were first born, those male children that were healthy were initiated to a lifelong process of developing military savvy.

After you have your list, the next step is to prioritize your list. You want to go item by item and determine which is the most important item and progressively work your way down to the one that is the least important.

Going back to the previous example, I prioritized the list as follows:

1. Start a saving account for school expenses.
2. Research the colleges for academic programs, the cost of tuition, and so on.

3. Identify colleges that I am interested in.
4. Contact the admissions office.
5. Schedule an appointment with an admissions representative.
6. Identify student loan or scholarship options.
7. Get copies of my transcripts from my previous schools.
8. Obtain a college catalog.

My logic is as follows:
1. As soon as I have the thought of returning to school, I need to start saving.
2. Researching colleges come second so that I can compare programs and cost.
3. I then need to identify the college that I am interested in.
4. Next, I need to contact the admission office.
5. I need to schedule an appointment with the admissions representative so that I can get my questions answered and receive relevant information.
6. I would then follow-up on financial assistance, order transcripts, and then get a catalog.

Scheduling your Goals

When you have your list prioritized, the next step is to use a calendar or planner to schedule each item on your list. Some items which take a single action can be scheduled as is while those items that involve multiple tasks can be broken down further into even smaller tasks. For example, ordering transcripts or getting a catalog is a single task item that can be scheduled as is. Researching colleges can involve multiple tasks. For example, what resources do I need in order to research the college? Do I need the internet? If I do not have the internet, do I know where I can get access to it? Once I started researching the colleges, do I know what I am researching for? Perhaps I need to make a list of all the things that I need to research in order to avoid wasting time or having to conduct the research a second time because I missed something.

Psychology of Goal Setting

We have just covered the mechanics of goal setting; however, there is another part of goal setting that is just as important, if not more, and that is the emotional aspect. Generating motivation, dealing with obstacles, and feedback are a crucial aspect for achieving goals. They are the equivalent of jet fuel for propelling us forward.

Having a goal is not enough if the passion is not there to see it through its completion. Once you have created a goal, you need to create a lasting level of emotional intensity for pursuing it. Without emotional intensity, it is easy to fall prey to self-doubt or give in to obstacles.

The following are two methods for maximizing the emotional meaning that you associate with your goals, legacy and taking ownership.

Legacy

The sense of legacy was ingrained in Spartans from a very early age. Children, especially boys, were taught that serving the state was the highest priority in their life. For this reason, Spartan warriors were fearless in battle and believed losing their life while fighting was most admirable.

If we can understand the deeper reason behind why we want to achieve our goals, we will be more likely be successful in achieving them. We want to ask ourselves the question "What would achieving this goal mean to me?" When trying to understand what achieving our goal would mean to us, we want to understand it from both an immediate and long-term perspective. We want to know how, if we met our goals today, how our life may be different tomorrow, five years from now, ten years from now, 20 years from now, and so on.

Exercise:

Write down your goals and, for each one, determine the fundamental reason for wanting to achieve it. In order to uncover your fundamental reason, continuously ask yourself "Why is that important to me?" or "What would that mean to me?"

For example, if my goal was to go back to school, my line of questioning might go like this:

1. "Why is going back to school important to me?"
   Answer: "I would be more marketable."
2. "Why is being more marketable important to me?
   Answer: I will be able to attract a larger income and get a better position."
3. What would a larger income and better position mean to me?
   Answer: I would be able to take better care of my family.

4. What would the ability to take better care of my family mean to me?
   Answer: I would know that I made a difference in their lives.

The driving reason behind the goal of returning to school is that I want to know that I made a difference in my family's life. This is a much stronger motivation for returning to school than "I would be more marketable."

By developing meaning for your goals, you will more likely to persevere in your actions until you achieve them. Having a strong enough reason for success is essential for success.

Taking ownership

When in battle, each Spartan warrior realized that how he conducted himself on the battlefield would have ramifications for all his comrades and the state of Sparta as a whole. The Spartan warrior took ownership for his actions. Research in goal setting has described what is known as the endowment effect, the power of taking ownership. The endowment effect refers to when our sense of ownership reaches the level such that the object of our interest becomes integrated with our sense of identity.

When we feel as though we own something, we are less likely to give it up. This goes back to the mental forces of perceived pain and pleasure. Many people have a greater fear of loss than a desire to gain something new. This is because we have a sense of certainty in that which we own but a sense of uncertainty in that which we have yet to obtain. An example of this is the person who is in a relationship or a job that they are not satisfied with, yet they fear to leave the relationship or job for a new one. While a new relationship or job may seem appealing, it remains an abstract idea, while the current job or relationship is something that they can be certain of.

For the people of Sparta, their state was a very large part of their identity, which is why the men were so fierce on the battlefield. When you have identified your goals, take the time to reflect on how you can tie them to your sense of identity. This is why the sense legacy, as previously described, is so powerful when striving to accomplish a goal.

Exercise:

Reflect on how your goal is directly or indirectly tied to your sense of identity. For example, we all have heard of parents who toil away for years at a job that they did not necessarily enjoy. They did it because they wanted their children's lives to be better than theirs. In this case, it is the love for their children that kept them going. Another example is the person who experiences a life-changing moment, resulting in a change of their priorities. Because of this, they become a completely new person with a whole new focus on life. An example is the gang member who takes the life of an innocent person. Because of the tragedy, they commit their life to peace by speaking out against violence.

Obstacles

Whenever we try to move forward with our life, we are bound to encounter obstacles. Obstacles are a primary reason for why most people do not accomplish their goals. But the encountering of obstacles is a given. Anytime you attempt to move forward in life; you are bound to experience resistance.

The key to dealing with obstacles is to have the understanding that they are a natural part of the process of pursuing goals. Further, obstacles are not a negative, in fact, they support us. How may you ask? Because growth is a fundamental and essential aspect of everything, that exists within this universe. Whether it is the expansion of the universe or a single cell dividing, life is about growth. In order for growth to occur; however, there must be obstacles or resistance. If everything in your life were absolutely perfect, there would be no reason for growth and a lack of growth results in stagnation.

Obstacles are the stimulus for a creative response by a biological organism. By developing an effective response, the organism can overcome the obstacle; it is the overcoming of the obstacle that spurs growth. When it is ready to emerge from its egg, a chick needs to chip its way through the egg shell. If the chick can not do so, it will die. If it can escape the confines of its egg, its growth will continue to progress. Despite the fact that the Spartan army was smaller than many of its neighbors, the discipline of its individual soldiers made it possible to conquer neighboring countries.

Exercise:

Make a list of all the potential obstacles you could encounter while pursuing your goals. Beside each obstacle, come up with ideas of how you would address it should it appear.

Procrastination

Why is it that Spartan warriors rushed toward the enemy while some of us avoid taking out the trash, getting in shape, or following through our New Year's resolutions? The Spartan's lifestyle was very effective in warding off procrastination. Spartan life was very effective in manipulating the forces that lead to procrastination, that of pain and pleasure.

Procrastination is simply the result of us being hardwired to avoid aversive situations and pursue that which we believe will lead to a greater state of happiness. This dynamic is actually a survival mechanism that allows a living organism to avoid life-threatening situations while moving toward situations that support survival.

Unfortunately, we have allowed this mechanism for survival to encompass even the most mundane activities, such as taking out the trash. For those of us who procrastinate taking out the trash, the internal dialogue that we engage in goes something like this: "Taking out the trash is a hassle, and it is so relaxing just to lie here on the couch. I will just take it out later." This kind of thinking then gradually expands until it encompasses more and more aspects of our life. Soon, the stakes become higher, and we find ourselves procrastinating on taking action on those matters that have a greater impact on our life such as finding a new job, paying off our debt, taking better care of our health, saving for retirement, and improving our relationships.

We procrastinate on such activities due to fear of failure, fear that taking action will be too difficult, or fear of the unknown, the unknown of what will happen if we achieve our goal. Regardless of what the fear is, it is the cause of procrastination.

Exercise:
Besides understanding the "Why" behind your decision to pursue a goal, a great way to avoid procrastination is to amp up the cost and benefits of achieving or not achieving your goal.

1. Get a piece of full-size notebook paper and fold it in half lengthwise.

2. On the top of the paper, write out your goal.

3. On the left side of the paper, write down a list of all the consequences that you have experienced in the past due to procrastinating. Also, think of all the consequences you may experience in the future, if you continue to procrastinate. When doing this exercise, it is important to write from your heart, not your head. Write down anything that comes to mind. Also, try to write nonstop.

4. When you have completed your list, repeat this exercise, only this time you will write a list of all the benefits that you will receive if you achieve your goal. Make your list as long as possible.

5. When writing, it is important to allow yourself to experience the emotions that come up. This exercise is intended to be experienced at the level of emotions as this is where procrastination takes holds. Reread your lists in the morning and in the evening before going to bed. When reading the lists, try to feel the emotions that come up with each item. Read your lists each day until you

become fully associated with the feelings that are related to achieving your goal as well as with those feelings of not succeeding.

Feedback

We have discussed the mechanics of setting goals as well as the emotional aspect. These two aspects are like the twin jets of a rocket. The mechanics set the course of the rocket and the emotional aspect is what propels the rocket. However, that is not enough. For the rocket to remain on course and hit its target, it needs a third aspect, feedback.

When a rocket is in flight, constant adjustments need to be made in order to keep it on the course. Similarly, you need constant feedback on how you are progressing toward your goal. Feedback informs you as to whether you are moving in the right direction, just as the scoreboard informs an athlete of his or her performance. Further, it informs you as to the type of adjustments that you need to make in order to get back on track. The following are two powerful ways for obtaining feedback. I recommend you use both:

1. Find someone who has already accomplished the goal that you are striving for and ask them if you can use them as a mentor. Let them know on a weekly basis of the action you have taken and the results that you received.

2. Review daily your plan for your goals as well as your scheduling of tasks. Ask yourself how well are you following through with what you scheduled and planned.

"Son, remember your courage with each step."

(A Spartan mother to her son.)

FIVE

Developing your Master Plan for Achieving your Goals

We have covered a lot of information in this book, so in this chapter, we will connect all this information to create your master plan for achieving your goal.

Your first step is to review Chapter 3. Carefully reflect on the 8 Spartan principles. Decide on which of these principles you could improve on that would help you in your achievement of your goals.

This first step is one of the most important steps that you can take in this book, perhaps even more important than the goals that you have set for yourself. Hopefully, you will set goals for yourself all of your life. But who you are is more than your goals; your goals are just an expression of who you are. More important than your goals is who you become as a person.

Who you are as a person will express itself in everything you do. In fact, if you did nothing else but practice the cultivation of the eight principles, you would most likely achieve your goals anyway. So decide which principles would benefit you the most and practice them each day until they become a part of you. This first step has no due date; make practicing these principles a lifelong project. As you practice the principles, your next step for achieving your goals is to assess your goals (see Chapter 4). Identify the major areas of your life and rate each one as to your level of fulfillment.

Your second step is to create your goals. Remember, when developing your goals, it is important that you meet the following criteria:
- Level of Difficulty
- Written
- Specific
- Measurable
- Timeline

For your third step, you want to turn your goals into outcomes; you want to get a vision for what your goals would look like if they were actualized today. You want to make this vision as vivid as possible, and you want to engage this vision with as many of you five senses as possible. You want to see it, hear it, and feel it. You want to take time each day to practice experiencing your outcome being fully realized.

The combination of well-crafted goals and visualizing the outcome of them will make your goals become a focal point of your consciousness. When this happens, you will experience the people, situations, and events coming into your life that will support you in achieving your goals.

The fourth step processes. Brainstorm all the things that you need to do or learn in order to achieve your goals. Remember to make this list as long as possible, and write down anything that comes to mind. When you have your list, prioritize each item from the most important to the least.

Your final step is scheduling your items from step four and making a commitment that you will handle them.

At this point, you have completed the first half of the master plan. You have identified the principles that you want for your life, and you have developed your goals. You also worked through the outcomes and process. While you are actively carrying out this first half of the plan, you need to condition yourself emotionally so that you can maintain your drive and focus as you execute your plan. In order to condition yourself for success, do the following:

Understand your legacy. You will find your legacy when you understand the ultimate "Why" behind your goals. When you understand the "Why," you will uncover your driving purpose that will keep you moving forward.

Taking ownership: The strongest force in the human condition is that of identity. When you can integrate your goals with your sense of identity, your goals will become part of you.

Obstacles: You are guaranteed to encounter obstacles as you pursue your goals. Be proactive and anticipate the potential barriers that you many encounter and determine how you will handle them.

A common obstacle is a procrastination. Procrastination is the result of the fear of moving toward your goals being greater than the pain of not changing. By listing the consequences for not achieving your goals and the benefits of achieving them, you can reverse these forces and make them work for you.

Finally, there is feedback. It is vital that you have a way to experience feedback as to whether you are moving closer toward your goals or not. There are numerous ways of receiving feedback and the way you receive feedback can differ with each goal. Two ways of receiving feedback that can be used with any goal are:

1. Find someone who has already accomplished the goal that you are striving for and ask them if you can use them as a mentor. Let them know on a weekly basis of the action you have taken and the results that you received.

2. Review daily your plan for your goals as well as your scheduling of tasks. Evaluate how well you

are following through with what you scheduled and planned.

"We don't rise to the level of our expectations, we fall to the level of our training." -Archilochus

Conclusion

One More Example

In conclusion, I would like to leave you with one more example of the epic journeys that Odysseus undertook. He and his men were sailing home, which involved passing by an island inhabited by sirens, mermaids whose seductive calls had lured many sailors to the island. Upon arriving on the island, the sirens would kill them. Understanding this, Odysseus had his men fill their ears with wax, which when hardened, would prevent them from hearing the sirens' calls.

Though he sealed his ears with wax as well, Odysseus ordered his men to take the additional step of tying him to the ship's masts. As they came within hearing distance of the sirens' calls, the wax in Odysseus's ears began to melt, allowing him to hear their them. Under the spell of the sirens' calls, Odysseus ordered his men to untie him so that he could seek the sirens out. Fortunately, his men could not hear his orders as the wax in their ears did not melt. Because of this, the Odysseus and his men safely sailed out of range of the sirens' calls.

Developing self-discipline is not easy, as you are bound to experience temptations that will lure you off course. Distractions are normal, and you will be enticed by them. What is most important is that you regain course and continue onward. In fact, you can learn self-discipline even if you never heard of these principles. Just challenging yourself just as Odysseus did will create the fertile grounds for self-discipline. The most important thing is that you be willing to take the journey.

"Don't let anything stop you! Work hard! Keep Pushing, and one day your words will be quoted by books as well!"
– Chris Thomson

Download Another Book for Free

I want to thank you for buying my book. I am offer you another book (just as awesome as this book), Mental Toughness Develop a Winner's Mindset and conquer success, totally free.

Go to the link below to receive it: http://bit.ly/2aBjMR7

In Mental Toughness, you will be introduced to a mindset that can assist you in tough times.

In addition to getting Mental Toughness, you will also have the opportunity my new books for free, enter giveaways, and receive other valuable emails from me. Again here is the link to sign up: http://bit.ly/2aBjMR7

Notes

Someday is not a day of the week. -Denise Brennan-Nelson

Notes

"To succeed...You need to find something to hold on to, something to motivate you, something to inspire you."- Tony Dorsett

Notes

"It isn't the mountains ahead to climb that wear you out; it's the pebble in your shoe."-Muhammad Ali

Notes

"Wisdom is always an overmatch for strength."-Phil Jackson

Notes

"Know yourself and you will win all battles."- Lao Tzu

Notes

"Nobody can make you feel inferior without your consent."-
Eleanor Roosevelt

Notes

"Toughness is in the soul and spirit, not in muscles."- Alex Karras

Notes

"Don't carry your mistakes around with you. Instead, place them under your feet and use them as stepping stones to rise above them." - Ryan Ferreras

Notes

"It's not so much about how things turn out, but how we conduct ourselves through our trials" ~Seth M. Quealy

Notes

*"He who is not everyday conquering some fear has not learned
the secret of life" - Ralph Waldo Emerson*

Notes

"Your time is limited, so don't waste it living someone else's life." -Steve Jobs